PHOTOGRAPHS: DINO SASSI
Interior photographs of the White House,
pages 67 & 68, copyright White House Historical Association
Photographs by National Geographic Society.

Starplex, page 84, photograph by Jim Doane
Pentagon, page 91, photograph by Harold Flecknoe/Uniphoto

DESIGN: DINO SASSI
Graphic consultant: Renzo Matino

© 1981 **KINA Italia S.p.A.** - MILAN/ITALY
Published by **L.B. Prince** Co., Inc.
8900 Lee Highway
Fairfax, Virginia 22031
1st Edition April, 1981
2nd Edition January, 1982
3th Edition June, 1983
4th Edition January, 1985

Full color lithography by KINA Italia S.p.A., Piazza Aspromonte 13, 20131 Milan, Italy

WASHINGTON, D.C.

In less than 200 years one of the world's most beautiful capital cities has emerged from what was virtually nothing more than a marshy wilderness. Containing the central governmental seat of a prosperous and powerful nation, Washington, D.C. has been the Capital of the United States' government since 1800. The plans for it were begun in 1791 when the first President of the United States, George Washington, selected this site, and then chose Pierre Charles L'Enfant as the man to design the city. Paris-born L'Enfant was an engineer in the Continental Army and his sweeping design for the Capital City was patterned in part on the splendid expanses of Versailles.

The efforts of Thomas Jefferson and Alexander Hamilton were extremely instrumental during the controversy of a proposed site for the Capital. Many previous attempts to select a place failed owing to the political rivalry between the states, and between 1783 and 1790, Congress considered various sites for the new Nation's capital, but was unable to reach an agreement. At one time they authorized work on a site near Trenton, New Jersey; later chose Germantown, Pennsylvania, and in the meantime, settled down in Philadelphia, Pennsylvania as a temporary capital. By 1790, feelings were so strong over the issue of where the Capital was to be located, that the South threatened Wisely, Jefferson and Hamilton reached a compromise: Jefferson would endorse Hamilton's proposal for Federal Government assumption of State war debts, if Hamilton would endorse a site on the Potomac for the new capital. Both bills passed, and President Washington was able to make his selection. He decided upon a site of 10 square miles lying on both sides of the Potomac River. The northern part was ceded by Maryland and the southern by Virginia. Later, the southern portion was returned to Virginia and became the city of "Washington" (as it was known at the time). "Territory of Columbia".

Pierre Charles L'Enfant planned and designed the city with great foresight. L'Enfant selected Capitol Hill as the focal point and laid out broad avenues which radiate like the spokes of a wheel from centers placed within the rectangular pattern of the streets. Although L'Enfant's handsome plan was is the end changed a great deal, his wide avenues and sweeping vistas combined with monumental buildings make the Capital unique among American Cities.

On August 24, 1814, during the War of 1812, the British took the city and over the next few days burned all of the public buildings except the combined post and patent offices. The White House was rebuilt by 1817 and two years later the Capitol Building again was ready for use.

In its early days, the city centered around Lafayette Square, reaching east to the Capitol and west to old Georgetown. Many of the colonial houses are still standing in these areas and many more well worth seeing, can be found in nearby Virginia. Now the Capital reflects various styles of architectural design, although most of it conforms to the classical Greek and Roman. Its imposing buildings are seldom over four or five stories in height and hundreds of monuments and memorials honor the heroes and statesmen of America and its allies. Noted for its art galleries and museums, there are now legitimate theaters, and a fine symphony orchestra. With few exceptions, most of the great landmarks are only a short distance apart.

The city's population has grown rapidly. In 1840 it was 44,000 and by 1860 the population had reached 75,000. Today, Washington has a population of over 750,000 about two-thirds of which work for the Federal Government.

In 1900, Washington celebrated the 100th Anniversary of the removal of the seat of Government to the District of Columbia. The population then was 278,218. Cable cars were being replaced by electric cars and horse drawn vehicles were giving way to automobiles. Railroad tracks still lay on the Mall and the sites of the Lincoln and Jefferson Memorials were a swamp land. William McKinley was President and Theodore Roosevelt was Vice-President. The District at that time had a veterinarian on its payroll as there were 500 horses and mules in service.

As L'Enfant has planned, Washington has vast acreages of parks, squares, circles and open space. While it is important as the center of the U.S. Federal Government, it is also a great cultural center containing numerous museums, art galleries, libraries, shrines, churches, parks and monumental buildings. It is no wonder that each year, millions of visitors from all parts of the world come to see this magnificent city, less than 200 years old, but already so richly endowed with beauty and American history.

WASHINGTON, D.C.

L'une des plus belles villes-capitale au monde; elle a été créé en moins de 200 ans sur une terre virtuellement marécageuse et inculte. Siège central gouvernemental d'une nation florissante et puissante, Washington, D.C. est la Capitale du Gouvernement des Etats Unis depuis l'année 1800. Les plans de la Ville avaient été commencés en 1791 après que le premier Président des Etats Unis, George Washington, avait choisi cet emplacement et avait chargé Pierre Charles L'Enfant de tracer les plans de la ville. Né à Paris, L'Enfant était ingénieur dans l'Armée Continentale; il s'inspira, en partie, pour son projet d'ensemble des splendides étendues de Versailles.

Les efforts de Thomas Jefferson et l'Alexandre Hamilton étaient extrêmement pragmatiques au cours de la polémique qui enfiévra les esprits au sujet du choix de l'emplacement de la capitale. Plusieurs tentatives précédentes échouèrent à cause de la rivalité politique qui divisait les états et, dans la période comprise entre 1783 et 1790, le Congrès examina divers emplacement sur lesquels la capitale de la jeune nation pouvait être bâite sans toutefois arriver à un accord. A un moment donné le Congrès autorisa d'entreprende les travaux dans une région située à proximité de Trenton, dans le New Jersey, puis il porta son choix à Germantown, en Pennsylvanie, et s'installa, entretemps, à Philadelphie, Pennsylvanie, qui devint la Capitale provisoire. En 1790 les esprits étaient tellement échauffés su sujet de la décision qui devai être prise quant à l'emplacement de la capitale, que le Sud menaça la sécession. Sagement Jefferson et Hamilton arrivèrent à un compromis: Jefferson acceptait la proposition de Hamilton qui demandait que le Gouvernement Fédéral prenne à sa charge les dettes de guerre de l'Etat, à condition que Hamilton appuyât le choix d'un emplacement de la nouvelle capitale sur le Potomac. Les deux décrets passèrent au Congrès, furent votés et le Président Washington put enfin faire son choix. Il opta pour une terre de 10 milles carrés qui s'étendait des deux côtés du Fleuve Potomac. La partie nor était cédée par le Maryland et la partie sud par la Virginie. Plus tard, la portion sud était restituée à la Virginie et le ''Territoire de Columbia'' (comme on l'appelait à l'époque) devint la Ville de Washington.

Pierre Charles L'Enfant étudia le projet et traça les plans de la Ville avec une claire vision de l'avenir. Il choisit Capitol Hill comme point central et il dessina de larges avenues qui partaient en étoile comme les rayons d'une roue, de centres placés à l'intérieur du quadrilatère qui formait les rues. Malgré d'importantes modifications qui furent apportées par la suite à son plan, ses larges avenues t ses profondes échappées, ses constructions monumentales font, de cette Capitale, une ville unique en Amérique.

Le 24 Août 1814, pendant la guerre de 1812, les Anglais prirent la ville et brûlèrent, au cours des jours qui suivirent, tous les édifices publics à l'exception du bâtiment qui logeait les bureaux de la poste et des brevets. La Maison Blanche fut reconstruite en 1817 et deux ans plus tard le Capitole était de nouveau terminé et disponible.

Au début, la ville était concentrée autour du Square Lafayette et atteignait, à l'est, le Capitole et, à l'ouest, la vieille Georgetown. Bon nombre de maisons coloniales sont encore debout dans ces zones et d'autres, bien plus nombreuses intéressantes à visiter, peuvent être découvertes d'architecture variés avec une certaine prépondérance du style Grec et Romain classique. Ses édifices, imposants, dépassent rarement quatre ou cinq étages et des centaines de monuments commémoratifs honorent les héros et les hommes d'Etat de l'Amérique et de ses alliés. Outre ses galeries d'art et ses musées alle offre aujourd'hui des salles de spectacles consacrées et un excellent orchestre symphonique. A part quelques rares exceptions, la plupart des centres d'intérêt sont concentrés dans des zones rapprochées.

La population de la ville s'est rapidement accrue. En 1840 elle était de 44.000 habitants, en 1860 sélevait à 75.000. Aujourd'hui Washington compte plus de 750.000 habitants dont les deux tiers environ travaillent pour le Gouvernement Fédéral.

En 1900 Washington célébra le centième Anniversaire du transfert du Siège du Governement dans le District de Columbia. La population s'élevait, à cette époque, à 278.718 habitants. Les trams, qui trainés par câble, étaient remplacés par les trams électiques et les véhicules trainés par des chevaux faisaient place aux automobiles. Les rails dans le Mall existent encore et les monuments commémoratifs de Lincoln et Jefferson se dressaient, alors, sur un terrain marécageux. William McKinley était Président et Théodore Roosevelt Vice-Président. Le District avait, à cette époque, un vétérinaire public car 500 chevaux et mulets étaient de service.

Conformément au plan de L'Enfant, Washington possède de vastes zones de parcs, squares, places et espaces ouverts. Importante comme céntre du Governement Fédéral des Etats Unis, Washington est aussi un grand centre culturel grâce à ses nombreux musées, galeries d'art, bibliothèques, chapelles, églises, parc et constructions monumentales. Il n'est pas étonnant que des millions de touristes provenant de toutes les parties du monde viennent visiter, tous les ans, cette ville magnifique, qui n'est pas encore bicentenaire mais déjà si riche en beautés et impregnée d'histoire Américaine.

WASHINGTON, D.C.

In weniger als 200 Jahren entstand hier eine der schonsten Stadte der Welt, wo davor praktisch nichts anderes als unwegsame Wildnis herrschte. Als zentraler Regierungssitz einer blühenden und mächtigen Nation ist Washington seit dem Jahre 1800 die Hauptstadt der Regierung der Vereinigten Staaten. Die Pläne zu der Stadtgründung gehen zurück auf das Jahr 1791, wo George Washington, der erste Präsident der Vereinigten Staaten, den Ort ausgewählt hatte; danach beauftragte er Pierre Charles L'Enfant mit der Planung der Stadt. Der in Paris gebürtige L'Enfant was Ingenieur in der Europäischen Armee und sein überwältigender Entwurf fur diese Hauptstadt war stark geprägt von den weitläufigen Ausmassen von Versailles.

Die Zusammenrbeit von Thomas Jefferson und Alexander Hamilton war äusserst zweckmässig, zumal hinsichtlich der Wahl des Ortes für die zu errichtende Hauptstadt grosse Meinungsverschiedenheiten bestanden. Alle früheren Versuche, einen geigneten Platz auszuwählen, scheiterten an der Rivalitätspolitik der einzelnen Staaten untereinander; in den Jahren zwischen 1783 und 1790 schlug der Kongress etliche etliche Plätze für die neue Hauptstadt vor, aber es konnte keine Eingung erzielt werden. Einmal hatte man sich fast bereits für ein Gebiet in der Nähe von Trenton in New Jersey entoschlossen, ein andermal dachte man an Germantown in Pennsylvania - während sich in der Zwischenzeit notgedrungenerweise eine Art Hauptstadt in Philatelphia, Pennsylvania, vorläufig bildete. Im Jahre 1790, als man immer noch zu keiner Einigung gelangt war, wo nun denn die neue Hauptstadt anzusiedeln sei, drohte der Süden mit seiner Loslösung von der Union. Klugerweise gelangten dann Jefferson und Hamilton zu einer Einigung: Jefferson akzeptierte Hamilton's Vorschlag, die Staatskriegsschulden durch die Bundesregierung tilgen zu lassen, vorausgesetzt, dass Hamilton der Gründung der nuenen Hauptstadt am Potomac Fluss zustimmen wurde. Beide Vorschläge wurden angenommen, sodass Präsident Washington nun seinen Voeschlag zur Ortswahl ducchsetzen konnte. Er entschied sich fur eine Fläche von über 10 Quadratmeilen beiderseits des Potomac Flusses. An dieses Areal grenzte in Norden Maryland und im Süden Virginia. Später wurde der südliche Teil an Virginia zurückerstattet und das "Territorial von Columbia" - als solches was es damals bekannt - wurde nun die Stadt Washington.

Pierre Charles L'Enfant hatte die Stadt in weiser Voraussicht geplant und entworfen. L'Enfant hatte den kapitolinischen Hügel als Brennpunkt auserwählt, von dem aus breite Alleen und Prachtstrassen wie die Speichen eines Rades gehen, die sich harmonisch dem rasterartigem Strassensystem einorden lassen. Obwohl L'Enfants Entwurf letztlich groben Veränderungen unterworfen wurde, bildet die Hauptstadt mit ihren grosszügigen Prachtstrassen und Denkmälern eine Einheit bilden, eine einzigartige Ausnahme unter den amerikanischen Städten.

Am 24. August 1814, mitten im Krieg von 1812, eroberten die Engländer die Stadt und brannten innerhalb weniger Tage sämtliche öffentliche Gebäude mit Ausnahme des Bürobaues der Post und des Patentamtes nieder. Das Weisse Haus wurde im Jahre 1817 wieder aufgebaut und zwei später konnte auch das Kapitol wieder bezogen werden.

In der ersten bestehenszeit bildete der Lafayette Platz das Stadzentrum, das sich im Osten bis zum Kapitol und im Westen zum alten Georgetown erstreckte. Noch heute bedinden sich in dieser Gegend viele Häuser im Kolonialstil, und noch viele mehr und wirklich sehenswerte kann man heute noch in Virginia finden. Heute spiegelt die Hauptstadt viele architektonische Stile wieder, aber die meisten halten sich an die griechische und römische Klassik. Seine Kollossalbauten ragen nur selten über die Höhe von vier oder fünf Stockwerken empor; hunderte von Monumenten und Gedächtnisstätten ehren die Helden und Staatsmänner von Amerika und seinen Verbündeten. Es ist bekannt für seine Kunstgalerien und Museen und verfügt heute über selbständige Theaterkompanien und ein ausgezeichnetes Symphonieorchester. Mit nur ganz wenigen Ausnahmen sind sämtliche wichtigen Landesgrenzen nur unbedeutend entfernt.

Die Stadbevölkerung ist rapid gewachsen. Während es im Jahr 1840 noch 44.000 Einwohner zählte, war man um 1860 bereits auf eine Zahl von 75.000 gelangt. Heute zählt Washington mehr als 750.000 Einwohner, von denen ungefähr zwei Drittel für die Bundsregierung arbeiten.

Im Jahre 1900 feierte Washington den hundersten Jahrestag der Zugestehung des Regierungssitzes im Bezirk von Columbia. Damals zahlte die Bevölkerung ca. 278.718 Einwohner. Pferdestrassenbahnen wurden durch elektrische Tramways ersetzt, und die privaten Pferdegespanne und Kutschen mussten dem Automobil weichen. Noch heute kann man die Strassenbahnschienen am Mall und in der Nähe der Denkmäler Lincoln's und Jefferson's entdecken. Dahinter herrschte damals freies Land. William McKinley war damals Präsident und Theodore Roosevel erfüllte seine Pflicht als Vizepräsident. Die Gemeinde musste damals einen Tierarzt erhalten und es gab über 500 Pferde und Maultiere im Dienst.

Der Planung L'Enfant's getreu verfügt Washington auch noch heute über riesige Parkflächen, Plätze, baumbestandene Rundflächen und Grünanlagen. Es ist nicht nur als Riegierungssitz der Bundesregierung der Vereinigten Staaten von immenser Bedeutung, sondern auch als kulturelles Zentrum mit seinen zahlreichen Museen, Kunstgalerien, Bibliotheken, Mausoleen, Kirchen, Parkanlagen und Monumentalbauten. So ist es kein Wunder, dass jedes Jahr Millionen von Besuchern von allen Teilen der Welt angereist kommen, um diese herrliche Stadt kennenzulernen, die trotz ihres jungen Bestehens von weniger als 200 Jahren bereits so reich mit Schönheit und amerikanischer Geschichte gesegnet ist.

WASHINGTON, D.C.

En menos de 200 años, una de las ciudades capitales más bellas del mundo ha emergido de lo que no era virtualmente más que un desierto pantanoso. Conteniendo la sede central del gobierno de una nación próspera y poderosa, Washington, D.C. ha sido la Capital del gobierno de los Estados Unidos desde 1800. Los planes para ello fueron comenzados en 1791 cuando el primer Presidente de los Estados Unidos, George Washington, escogió este lugar, y luego designó a Pierre Charles L'Enfant como al hombre que habría de diseñar la ciudad. L'Enfant, nacido en París, era un ingeniero en el Ejército Continental y su diseño en esquema para la Ciudad Capital estaba inspirado en parte en los espléndidos espacios de Versailles.

Los esfuerzos de Thomas Jefferson y de Alexander Hamilton fueron extremamente instrumentales durante la controversia acerca del lugar propuesto para la capital. Muchas intentonas precedentes de seleccionar un sitio habían fracasado a causa de las rivalidades políticas entre los estados y entre 1738 y 1790, el Congreso consideró varios lugares para situar en ellos a la capital de la Nación, per no fué capaz de llegar a un acuerdo. Una vez se autorizó el comienzo de los trabajos en un lugar cerca de Trenton, New Jersey; más tarde se escogió Germantown, Pennsylvania, y mientras tanto, se instalp en Philadelphia, Pennsylvania, como en una capital provisional. Hacia 1790, los ánimos estaban tan excitados respecto al éxito de la cuestión de donde se iba a localizar por fín a la capital, que el Sur amenazó una secesión por este motivo. Muy estutamente, Jefferson y Hamilton llegaron a un compromiso: Jefferson habría apoyado la propuesta de Hamilton para que el Gobierno Federal aceptase las deudas de guerra del Estado, si Hamilton apoyaba la elección de un lugar en el Potomac para la nueva capital. Lor dos proyectos de ley fueron aprobados, y el Presidente Washington pudo hacer su selección. Se decidió por un lugar de 10 millas cuadradas situado a ambas partes del Rio Potomac. La parte norte fué cedida por Maryland y la parte sur por Virginia. Más tarde, la parte sur se devolvió a Virginia y el "Territorio de Columbia" (como era conocido en aquella época), se convirtío en la ciudad de "Washington"

Pierre Charles L'Enfant hizo los planes y diseñó la ciudad con gran precisión. L'Enfant escogió la Colina del Capitolio como el punto focal y dispuso amplias avenidas que irradiaban como los radios de una rueda desde centros situados dentro del perímetro rectangular de las calles. Aunque el hermoso plano de L'Enfant fué bastante cambiado al final, sus amplias avenidas y sus panoramas extensos combinados con edificios monumentales hicieron de la Capital una ciudad única entre las Ciudades Americanas.

El 245 de Agosto de 1814, durante la guerra del 1812, los Ingleses tomaron la ciudad y durante los días siguientes quemaron todos los edificios públicos excepto las oficinas combinadas de correor y patentes. La Casa Blanca fué reconstruída hacia 1817 y dos años más tarde el Edificio del Capitolio estaba de nuevo listo para ser utilizado.

En sus primeros días, el centro de la ciudad se extendía alrededor de la Plaza de Lafayette, alcanzando al Este el Capitolio y al Oeste la vieja Georgetown. Muchas de las casas coloniales todavía están en pie en estas zonas y muchas otras, que valen más la pena de ser vistas, pueden encontrarse en las cercanías de Virginia. Actualmente la Capital refleja varios estilos de diseño aequitectónico, aunque la mayor parte de la misma se inspira en el diseño clásico Griego y Romano. Sus edificios imponentes tienen raramente menos de cuatro o cinco pisos de altura y centenares de monumentos y de placas conmemorativas honoran a los héroes y a los hombres de estado de América y de sus aliados. Ya conocida por sus galerías de arte y sus museos, ahora tiene también teatros válidos y una orquesta sinfónica excelente. Con pocas excepciones, la mayor parte de los grandes lugares se encuentran a poca distancia entre sí.

La población de la ciudad creció rápidamente. En 1840 era de 44.000 personas, y hacia 1860 la población había alcanzado la cifra de 75.000 habitantes. Hoy en día, Washington tiene una población de más de 750.000 personas, alrededor de dos tercios de las cuales trabajan para del Gobierno Federal.

En 1900, Washington celebró el Centenario del desplazamiento de la sede del Gobierno al Distrito de Columbia. La población entonces era de 278.718 habitants. Los tranvías movidos por tracción de cable estaban siendo sustituidos por tranvías elétricos, y los vehículos movidos por caballos empezaban a dejar el paso a los automóviles. Huellas de carriles quedan aún en el Mall y los sitios que ocupan los monumentos conmemorativos de Lincoln y de Jefferson eran un terreno pantanoso. William McKinley era el Presidente y Theodore Roosevelt era el Vicepresidente. El Distrito en aquella época tenía a un veterinario en su nómina de sueldos ya que había entonces 500 caballos y mulos en servicio.

Gomo L'Enfant había planeado, Washington tiene muchos acres de parques, plazas, glorietas y espacio abierto. Así como es importante por ser el centro del Gobierno Federal de los Estados Unidos, es también un gran centro cultural que contiene numerosos museos, galerías de arte, bibliotecas, capillas, iglesias, parques y edificios monumentales. No sorprende que cada año, millones de visitantes de todas partes del mundo vengan a visitar esta magnífica ciudad, de menos de 200 años de antiguedad, pero ya tan ricamente dotada de belleza y de historia Americana.

The dome of the United States Capitol crowned with the Statue of Freedom.

La coupole du Capitole des Etats Unis couronnée par la Statue de la Liberté.

Die Kuppel des Kapitols der Vereinigten Staaten gekhönt von der Freiheitsstatue.

La Cúpula del Capitolio de los Estados Unidos coronada por la Estatua de la Libertad.

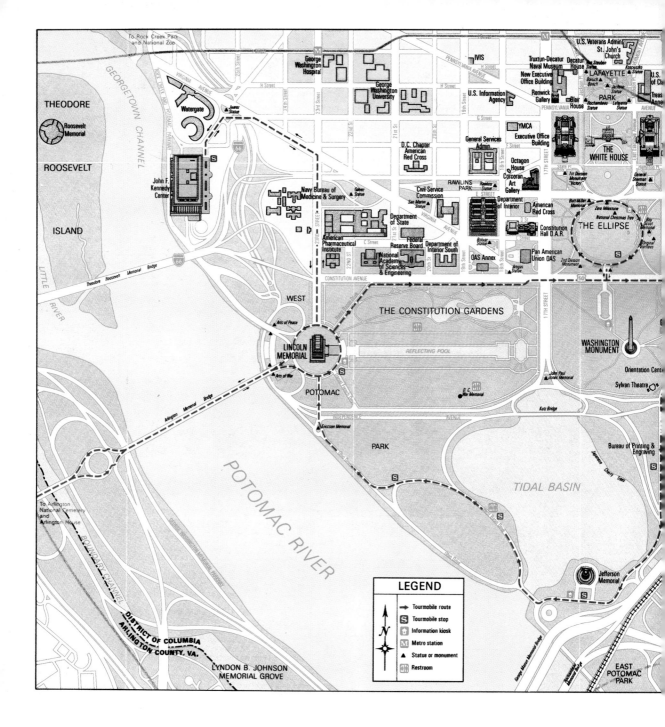

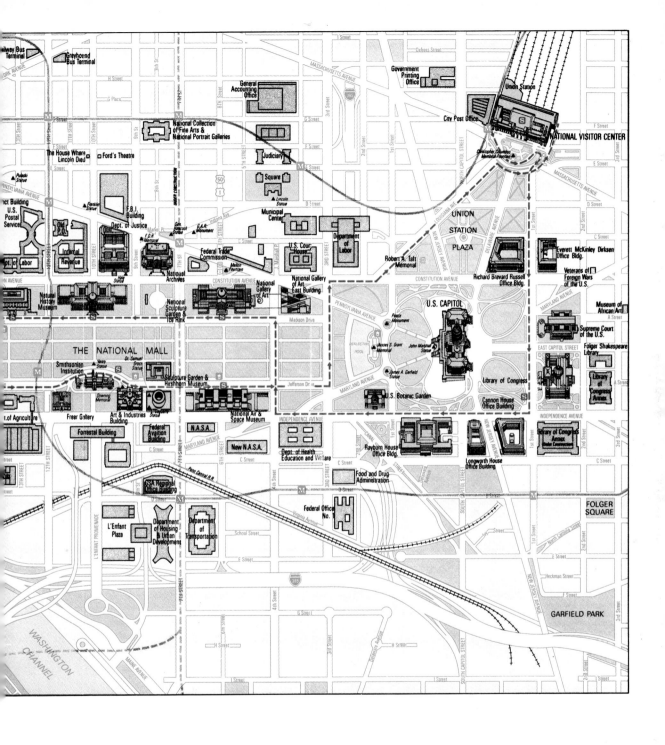

National Visitors Center/Historic Union Station. Designed by D.H. Burnham and completed in 1907, the architecture is Roman Classic. The front plaza is graced by a memorial to Christopher Columbus.

Nationales Besucherzentrum/Historischer Unionsbahnhof. Die architektonische Gestaltung erfolgte nach Entwuerfen des technischen Zeichners D.H. Burnham und wurde im Jahr 1907 im römisch-klassischen Stil beendet. Der davor befindliche grosse Platz wird durch ein Denkmal, das Christopher Columbus darstellt, gewuerdigt.

National Visitors Center/Historic Union Station. Dessinée par D.H. Burnham et achevée en 1907, l'architecture est de style Romain classique. Le devant de la place est embelli par le Mémorial à Christophe Colomb.

Centro de los Visitantes Nacionales/Estación de la Unión Histórica. Diseñada por D.H.Burnham y completada en 1907, el estilo arquitectónico es Clásico Romano. La plaza frontal está adornada por un monumento conmemorativo en honor a Cristobal Colón.

THE NATIONAL GUARD · THE NATION'S MINUTE MAN

President George Washington laid the cornerstone of the United States Capitol on September 18, 1793. The design for this impressive building resulted from a contest in which seventeen contestants submitted plans for the Capitol. The winner was an amateur designer, Dr. William Thornton. By 1827, the Capitol was completed according to his plans. Between 1851 and 1863, the Capitol was enlarged and a new dome was added. The east front was extended in 1958, but the original character of the building designed by Thornton has remained.

Präsident George Washington legte am 18. September 1793 den Grundstein des Kapitols der Vereinigten Staaten. Der Entwurf für dieses eindrucksvolle Gebäude war das Ergebnis eines Wettbewerbes, an dem siebzehn Teilnehmer ihre Ideen zur Ausgestaltung des Kapitols präsentierten. Gewinner war der Amateurzeichner Dr. William Thornton. Seinen Plänen getreu wurde das Kapitol im Jahre 1827 fertiggestellt. In den Jahren zwischen 1851 und 1863 wurde das Kapitol vergrössert und mit einer neuen Kuppel versehen. Im Jahre 1958 wurde die Ostseite erweitert, aber der von Thornton geprägte ursprüngliche Charakter des Gebäudes blieb dabei erhalten.

Le 18 Septembre 1793 le Président George Washington posa la première pierre du Capitole des Etats Units. Le plan de cet impressionnant bâtiment fut choisi parmi dix-sept autres, d'autant de concurrents qui avaient présenté leurs projets. Le gagnant était un dessinateur amateur, le Dr. William Thornton. En 1827 le Capitole était terminé conformément au plan original. Entre 1851 et 1863 il fut agrandi: un nouveau dôme lui fut ajouté et, en 1958, la façade Est fut agrandie; mais malgré ces modifications la construction a conservé son caractère original tel qu'il avait été conçu par Thornton.

El Presidente George Washington puso la piedra angular del Capitolio de los Estados Unitos el 18 de Septiembre de 1793. El diseño de este impresionante edificio era el resultado de una competición en la que diecisiete participantes habían presentado planos para el Capitolio. El ganador fué un dibujante aficionado, Dr. William Thornton. En 1827, el Capitolio estaba ya terminado siguiendo sus planos. Entre 1851 y 1863, el Capitolio fué ampliado y se le añadió una nueva cúpula. La fachada este se amplió en 1958, pero se ha conservado el carácter original del edificio proyectado por Thornton.

The Capitol is surrounded by a 68-acre park designed by Frederick Law Olmsted which includes many noble old trees, fountains and statues.

Le Capitole est entouré d'un parc qui s'étend sur 68 acres, dessiné par Frederick Law Olmsted; il contient un grand nombre de vieux et nobles arbres, des fountaines et statues.

Das Kapitol ist von einem 68 Acker (ca. 27 Hektar) grossen Park umgeben, der nach Plänen von Frederick Law Olmsted angelegt wurde. In diesem Park wachsen viele majestätische, alte Bäume und man findet etliche Springbrunnen und Steinfiguren.

El Capitolio está rodeado por un parque de 68 acres diseñado por Frederick Law Olmsted que contiene muchos viejos y nobles árboles, fuentes y estatuas.

e photograph at left lends witness to the interesting architectural
tailing which abounds at the Capitol.
n top of the Capitol Dome is the bronze figure of the Statue of Freedom
signed by the American artist Thomas Crawford. It was placed on the
me during the Civil War in 1863. It measures 19-feet, 6-inches in height
d weighs 14,985 pounds. The figure is of a woman with her right hand
a sheathed sword and her left holding a wreath, while clenching a
ield. Her unique helmet is encircled with stars and is composed of an
gle's head and feathers.

photographie à gauche montre des détails architecturaux intéres-
nts, nombreux au Capitole.
sommet du dôme du Capitole, la statue en bronze de la Liberté, réali-
e par l'artiste Américain Thomas Crawford. Elle fut placée sur le dôme
ndand la Guerre Civile en 1863. Son hauteur est de 19 pieds 6 pouces et
e pèse 14.985 livres. Elle représente une femme qui tient dans sa main
oite une épée avec garde et, dans sa main gauche, une couronne et serre
bouclier. Son casque, entouré d'étoiles, reproduit la tête d'un aigle et
s plumes.

e linke Photographie gibt Zeugnis von den interessanten architektoni-
hen Details, die in der Konstruktion des Kapitols reichlich vorhanden
nd.
n der Spitze der Kapitolskuppel befindet sich ein bronzenes Abbild der
eiheitsstatue, das von dem amerikanischen Künstler Thomas Crawford
tworfen worden ist. Sie wurde während des Bürgerkrieges im Jahre
63 auf die Kuppel montiert. Sie misst eine Höhe von 19 Fuss und 6 in-
es und wiegt 14.985 englische Pfund. Die Statue stellt eine Frau dar, die
ch mit der rechten Hand auf ein Schwert stützt und in der Linken ein
hild und einen Siegeskranz hält. Ihr einzigartiger Helm ist von Sternen
nkrönt und besteht aus einem Adlerkopf und Gefieder.

fotografía de la izquierda es una prueba de los interesantes detalles
quitectónicos que abundan en el Capitolio.
la cima de la Cúpula del Capitolio se encuentra la figura de bronce de
Estatua de la Libertad diseñada por el artista Americano Thomas
afword. Fué colocada sobre la cúpula durante la Guerra Civil en 1863.
de 19 pies y 6 pulgadas de altura y pesa 14.985 libras. La figura es la de
a mujer con la mano derecha sobre una espada envainada y la izquier-
sosteniendo una guirnalda mientras empuña un escudo. Su casco úni-
está rodeado de estrellas y está formado por la cabeza de un águila y
s plumas.

One of three House Office Buildings which accommodate the offices of the members of the House of Representatives.
One of two Senate Office Buildings where Members of the Senate have their offices. Both the House and Senate Office Buildings are conveniently connected with the Capitol by an underground subway system.

Un des trois bâtiments (House Office Building) où se trouvent les bureaux des membres de l'Assemblée Nationale.
Un des deux bâtiments du Sénat où se trouvent les bureaux des Sénateurs. Les édifices, tant de l'Assemblée que du Sénat, communiquent avec le Capitole par un système de passages souterrains.

Eines der drei Regierungsgebäude, die die einzelnen Büros der Abgeordneten beherbergen.
Eines der beiden Senatsbürogebäude, wo die Senatsmitglieder ihre Büros haben. Sowohl die Regierungs- wie auch die Senatsbüros sind mit dem Kapitol durch ein bequemes Untergrundbahnsystem verbunden.

Uno de los tres Edificios de Oficinas que contienen las oficinas de los miembros de la Casa de Representantes.
Uno de los dos Edificios de Oficinas del Senado donde los Miembros del Senado tienen sus oficinas. Tanto la Casa como los Edificios de Oficinas del Senado están oportunamente conectados con el Capitolio por medio de un sistema de metro.

Folger Shakespeare Library. Much of the spirit of Elizabethan England has been recreated here, including a replica of a Shakespearean theater and the greatest collection of the early editions of Shakespeare in the world.

La Bibliothèque Folger Shakespeare. L'esprit de l'Angleterre Elisabéthaine a été recréé ici, comprenant la reconstitution d'un théâtre Shakespearien et contenant la plus grande partie des premières éditions de Shakespeare qui existent dans le monde.

Die Bibliothek von Folger Shakespeare. Hier wurde viel vom Elisabethanischen Geist Englands nachempfunden; unter anderem befindet sich hier ein Modell eines Shakespeare-Theaters und die grösste Sammlung der frühen Shakespearausgaben in der ganzen Welt.

Biblioteca debida a Folger Shakespeare. Gran parte del espíritu de la Inglaterra de la época de Isabel I ha sido vuelto a crear aquí, incluyendo una copia del teatro de Shakespeare y la mayor colección de las primeras ediciones de Shakespeare del mundo.

Longworth House Office Building.

Le bâtiment Longworth House Office.

Das Longworth Bürogebaude.

Edificio de Oficinas de la Casa de Longworth.

The Capitol dome from afar.

Le dôme du Capitole vu de loin.

Fernansicht der Kapitolskuppel.

La cúpula del Capitolio desde lejos.

Supreme Court of the U.S. The temple-like, white marble structure was designed by Cass Gilbert and completed in 1935. The sculptured pediment represents "Liberty Enthroned" guarded by "Order" and "Authority".

La Cour Suprême des Etats Unis. La construction en marbre a la forme d'un temple; elle fut dessinée par Cass Gilbert et achevée en 1935. Le fronton sculpté représente "Liberté sur le Trône" protégée par "Ordre" et "Autorité".

Der Oberste Gerichtshof der Vereinigten Staaten. Diese tempelähnliche Architektur aus weissem Marmor wurde von Cass Gilbert entworfen und im Jahre 1935 fertiggestellt. Der gemeisselte Giebel stellt die "Freiheit auf dem Throne dar", die von der "Ordnung" und der "Autorität" bewacht wird.

La Corte Suprema de los EE.UU. El edificio con forma de templo, con estructura de mármol, fué diseñado por Cass Gilbert y completado en 1935. El frontón esculpido representa a la "Libertad Entronada" vigilada por el "Orden" y por la "Autoridad".

Library of Congress. The Library of Congress was established in 1800, and originally was located in the Capitol. The present massive building was completed in 1897 and shows the influence of the French Renaissance. It is completely decorated with excellent examples of 19th Century art.

Bibliothèque du Congrès. La bibliothèque du Congrès fut fondée en 1800; elle avait été installée, à l'origine, dans le Capitole. La construction actuelle, massive, fut achevée en 1897 et évoque l'influence de la Renaissance Française. Elle est complètement décorée d'excellents modèles de l'art du XIXème siècle.

Die Kongressbibliothek. Die Kongressbibliothek wurde im Jahre 1800 eingerichtet und war ursprünglich im Kapitol untergebracht. Das derzeitige massive Gebäude wurde im Jahre 1897 fertiggestellt und spiegelt den Einfluss der französischen Renaissance wieder. Es ist zur Gänze mit hervorragenden Kunstwerken aus dem neunzehnten Jahrhundert geschmückt.

Biblioteca del Congreso. La Biblioteca del Congreso fué establecida en 1800, y originariamente estaba situada en el Capitolio. El imponente edificio actual fué completado en 1897 y muestra la influencia del Renacimiento Francés. Está completamente decorado con excelentes ejemplares del arte del siglo XIX.

Robert A. Taft Memorial. This simple mo___
ment to the late Senator from Ohio was ded___
ted on April 14, 1959. The superbly matc___
French bells of the carillon frequently are ru___

Le Mémorial Robert A. Taft. Ce monument ___
lignes simples, élevé à la mémoire du Sénat___
de l'Ohio, fut consacré le 14 Avril 1959. Les ___
ches Françaises, superbes d'harmonie, c___
lonnent fréquemment.

Das Robert A. Taft Denkmal. Diese schlic___
Gedächtnisstaette wurde am 14. April 1___
dem späten Senator von Ohio gewidmet. ___
perfekt gestimmten Glocken des franz___
schen Glockenspiels werden häufig geläut___

Monumento a la Memoria de Robert A. T___
Este sencillo monumento dedicado al difu___
Senator de Ohio fué erigido el 14 de Abri___
1959. Las campanas francesas soberbiame___
emparejadas del carillón se tocan frecue___
mente.

The Washington Monument and Lincoln ___
morial from the Capitol. The towers of ___
structure at left are of the Smithsonian Inst___
tion, also known as the "Castle".

Le Monument à Washington et le Mémori___
Lincoln du Capitole. Les tours du bâtimen___
gauche sont celles de l'Institution Smith___
nienne; elles sont également connues com___
le "Château" (The Castle).

Das Washington Monument und die Linc___
Gedächtnisstätte vom Kapitol aus geseh___
Die Türme des linken Gebäudes gehören z___
Smithsonischen Institut, das auch unter d___
Spitznamen "Burg" bekannt ist.

El Monumento a Washington y el monume___
a la Memoria de Lincoln desde el Capito___
Las torres de la estructura a la izquierda ___
del Instituto Smithsoniano, y se las con___
también como el "Castillo".

In the Botanical Gardens there are regular a
changing displays which correspond to the s
sons of the year.

Dans les Jardins Botaniques, de régulières et
nouvelées expositions ont lieu, correspond
aux différentes saisons de l'année.

In den Botanischen Gärten finden der Saison e
sprechende regelmässige und ausserordentli
Blumenausstellungen statt.

En los Jardines Botánicos hay exposiciones pe
dicas y variadas que corresponden a las estad
nes del año.

National Air and Space Museum, dedicated to man's adventures in the conquest of air and space.

Musée National de l'Air et de l'Espace dédié aux aventures humaines pour la conquête de l'Air et de l'Espace.

Das Nationale Luftfahrt - und Weltraummuseum, dem Pioniergeist der Menschen zur Eroberung der Luft und des Weltraums gewidmet.

Museo Nacional del Aire y del Espacio, dedicado a las aventuras del hombre en la conquista del aire y del espacio.

Health, Education and Welfare Building.

Edifice de la Santé, de l'Education et de la Sécurité.

Das Ministerium für Gesundheit, Erziehung und Wohlfartswesen.

Edificio de la Salud, Educación y Bienestar.

Ulysses S. Grant Memorial

Mémorial Ulysses S. Grant.

Das Ulysses S. Grant Denkmal.

Monumento a la memoria de Ulysses S. Grant.

A view of Indépendance Avenue and the Depa
ment of Agriculture.

Une vue de l'Avenue Independence et le Dépar
ment de l'Agriculture.

Blick auf die Unabhängigkeits-Prachtstrasse u
auf das Landwirtschaftsministerium.

Una vista de la Avenida de la Independencia y
Departamento de la Agricultura.

Bureau of Engraving and Printing. Tours are co
ducted, during which visitors can see U.S. curre
cy being printed.

Bureau de la Gravure et de l'Impression. Des tou
réguliers sonto organisés pour les visiteurs,
cours desquels ceux-ci peuvent assister à l'i
pression des billets de banque U.S.

Die Staatsdruckerei. Hierher gibt es geführte To
ren, während denen die Besucher beim Druck
von amerikanischem Geld zusehen können.

Officina de Grabados e Imprenta. Se organizan e
cursiones, durante las cuales los visitantes pu
den ver como se acuña la moneda americana.

Smithsonian "Castle". The Smithsonian Institution, lovingly called "the nation's attic" was founded in 1846 under the terms of the will of James Smithson, an English scientist who had never crossed the Atlantic.

Smithsonian "Castle" (Château Smithsonien). L'Institution Smithsonienne, appelée affectueusement "mansarde de la Nation", fut fondée en 1846 conformément aux termes du testament de James Smithson, un savant Anglais qui n'avait jamais traversé l'Atlantique.

Die Smithsonische "Burg". Das Smithsonische Institut, in liebenswerter Weise auch die "Mansarde der Nation" genannt, wurde im Jahre 1846 dem letxten Willen von James Smithson entsprechend gegründet. Smithson war ein englischer Wissenschaftler, der selbst niemals den Atlantik überquert hatte.

El "Castillo" Smithsoniano. La Institución Smithsoniana, cariñosamente llamada "el ático de la nación", fué fundada en 1846 bajo las normas de la voluntad de James Smithson, un científico inglés que nunca había cruzado el Atlántico.

National Museum of Natural History and Museum of Man.
Of the 54 million articles in the museum's collection, usually only about one percent is ever on display at one time.

Le Musée National d'Histoire Naturelle et Musée de l'Homme.
Sur les 54 millions de pièces faisant partie de la collection du musée, rien que un pour-cent environ est exposé au même moment.

Das Naturhistorische und Völkerkundliche Nationalmuseum.
Von all den ca. 54 Millionen Stücken, die sich in dieser riesigen Sammlung befinden, wird für gewöhlich nur ein Prozent davon gleichzeitig ausgestellt.

Museo Nacional de Historia Natural y Museo del Hombre.
De los 54 milliones de artículos de la colección del museo, normalmente sólo aproxima-damente un uno por ciento está en exposición cada vez.

An exhibit in the National Museum of Natural History and Museum of Man.

Une exposition au Musée National d'Histoire Naturelle et Musée de l'Homme.

Ein Ausstellungsstück aus dem Naturhistorischen und Völkerkundlichen National-museum.

Una exposición en el Museo Nacional de Historia Natural y Museo del Hombre.

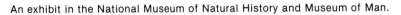

The National Zoological Park was established in 1890 for the purpose of preserving some of the animal life in North America that was threatened with extinction, but now includes some of the world's rarest animals.

Le Parc Zoologique National fut fondé en 1890 dans le but de protéger certains animaux en Amérique du Nord qui étaient en passe de disparaître; le Parc possède aujourd'hui quelques uns des animaux les plus rares au monde.

Der staatliche zoologische Garten wurde im Jahre 1890 errichtet, um manche nordamerikanische Tierarten zu erhalten, die vom Aussterben bedroht waren. Heutzutage beherbergt er allerdings einige der seltensten Tiere der ganzen Welt.

El Parque Zoológico Nacional fué establecido en 1890 con la finalidad de proteger a algunas especies animales de América del Norte que amenazaban la extinción, pero ahora incluye a algunos de los animales más raros del mundo.

Freer Gallery of Art. At the death of Charles L. Freer in 1919, his unusual collection of Far and Near Eastern art was given to the United States, along with a museum to house them.

Galcric d'Art Freer. A la mort de Charles L. Freer en 1919, sa collection exceptionnelle d'art de l'Extrême et du Proche-Orient fut léguée aux Etats Unis en même temps que le musée qui devait l'accueillir.

Die Freersche Kunstgalerie. Im Jahre 1919 - dem Todesjahr von Charles L. Freer - wurde seine ungewöhnliche Sammlung nah - und fernöstlischer Kunst den Vereinigten Staaten vermacht. Dazu wurde auch ein Museum gestiftet, das diese Sammlung beherbergt.

Galería de Arte Freer. Trás la muerte de Charles L. Freer en 1919, su insólita colección de arte del Cercano y Lejano Este fué regalada a los Estados Unidos, junto con un museo para alojarla.

Hirshorn Museum and Sculpture Garden. Financier Jospeph H. Hirshhorn contributed his collection of some 6000 paintings and sculptures in 1966 and the Smithsonian erected the circular building with a sunken sculpture garden to house the works.

Musée Hirshhorn et Jardin de la Sculpture. Le financier Joseph H. Hirshhorn fit don, en 1966, de sa collection qui comprenait 6000 tableaux de peinture et sculptures; l'Institution Smithsonienne construisit l'édifice circulaire où ces œuvres d'art furent exposées, doté d'un jardin en contrebas.

Das Hirshhorn Museum und der Skulpturengarten. Der Bankfachmann Joseph H. Hirshhorn leistete durch seine Schenkung von ca. 6000 Gemälden und Skulpturen im Jahre 1966 einen beachtlichen Beitrag. Die Smithsonische Stiftung errichtete diesen Rundbau und den darunter befindlichen Skulpturengarten, um diese Sammlung zu beherbergen.

Jardín de Esculturas y Museo Hirshhorn. El financiero Joseph Hirshhorn contribuyó con su colección de unos 6000 cuadros y esculturas en 1966 y los Smithsonianos erigieron el edificio circular con un jardín decorado con esculturas para alojar a las obras.

National Gallery of Art. The marble gallery and many of its great works were a gift made by financier Andrew Mellon in 1937. Since then, more than 200 donors have made additional contributions.

Galerie Nationale d'Art. La galerie de marbres et une grande partie de ses grandes œuvres furent offertes par le financier Andrew Mellon, en 1937. Depuis, plus de 200 donateurs ont apporté leur contribution.

Die Nationale Gemäldegalerie. Die Marmogalerie und viele der grossen Kunstwerke waren ein Geschenk des Bankfachmannes Andreas Mellon im Jahre 1937. Seit damals haben mehr als 200 Spender zusäzliche Beiträge geleistet.

Galería de Arte Nacional. La galería de mármol y muchas de sus grandes obras fueron un regalo ofrecido por el financiero Andrew Mellon en 1937. Desde entonces, más de 200 donantes han efectuado contribuciones adicionales.

The old Patent Office Building houses the [Na]tional Portrait Gallery and the National Col[lec]tion of Fine Arts.

L'ancien bâtiment des Bureaux de Brev[ets] abrite la Galerie Nationale du Portrait et la [Col]lection Nationale d'Art Fin.

Das alte Patentbüro beherbergt die Staatli[che] Portraitgalerie und die Staatliche Kunstsar[mm]lung.

El antiguo Eficicio de la Oficina de Paten[tes] aloja a la Galería Nacional de Retratos y [a la] Collección Nacional de Bellas Artes.

nwick Gallery. Its exhibits are of late Victorian interiors
d include American wood furniture, modern architecture
d industrial design.

lerie Renwick. Des vieux intérieurs de l'époque Victorien-
y sont exposés ainsi que des meubles en bois Améri-
ins, des pièces d'architecture moderne et des plans indu-
iels.

e Renwick Galerie. Die Exponate sind in der Hauptsache
äte viktorianische Innenräume und beinhalten ameri-
nische Holzmöbel, moderne Architektur und Industrie-
ojekte.

lería Renwick. Sus objetos pertenecen a decoraciones de
eriores de la época tarda victoriana e incluyen muebles
madera americana, arquitectura moderna y diseño indu-
ial.

National Air and Space Museum. On display here, you will find the "Spirit of St. Louis" and the Apollo Spacecraft.

Musée National de l'Air et de l'Espace. L'"Esprit de Saint Louis" et le Navire Spatial "Apollo" s'y trouvent exposés.

Nationales Luftfahrt- und Weltraummuseum. Hier findet man beispielsweise den "Geist von St. Louis" und die Apollo-Raumschiffe.

Museo Nacional del Aire y del Espacio. Expuestos aquí, encontrarán Vds. al "Spirit of St. Louis" y a la Nave Espacial Apollo.

Enjoying an ice cream "break" at the National Museum of History and Technology.

Jouissant d'un bref "entr'acte" au Musée National d'Histoire et Technologie, en savourant une glace.

Hier im Museum für Geschichte und Technologie kann man bei einem Eis eine Verschnaufpause einlegen.

Tomándose una "pausa" de helado en el Museo Nacional de Historia y Tecnología.

Federal Trade Commission Building. Two massive stone statues are on the eastern facade and depict man (the FTC) trying to control a horse (Trade). At right is the National Gallery of Art.

Bâtiment de la Commission Commerciale Fédérale. Deux grandes statues en pierre sur la façace est; elles représentent l'Homme (FTC - Federal Trade Commission) essayant de maîtriser un cheval (Commerce). A droite, la Galerie Nationale d'Art.

Das Burögebaude der Bundeskammer der Gewerblichen Wirtschaft. Die beiden gewaltigen Steinstatuen an der Ostfassade stellen einen Mann (die "Federal Trade Commission") dar, der ein Pferd (= Handel) zu bändigen versucht. Rechts davon befindet sich die Nationale Gemäldegalerie.

Edificio de la Comisión Federal de Comercio. Dos estatuas de piedra maciza se encuentran en la fachada este y representan a un hombre (la CFC) intentando controlar a un caballo (Comercio). A la derecha se encuentra la Galería Nacional de Arte.

The National Archives is the final repository for the permanent records of the U.S. Government.

Les Archives Nationales sont les dépôts où aboutissent finir les archives du Gouvernement des Etats Unis.

Das Staatsarchiv ist der letzte Aufbewahrungsort für die ewigen Erinnerungsstücke an die Regierung der Vereinigten Staaten.

El Archivo Nacional es el depósito final para los registros permanentes del Gobierno de los EE.UU.

Statue of General Winfield Scott.

Statue du Général Winfield Scott.

Das Denkmal von General Winfield Scott.

Estatua del General Winfield Scott.

upper left, Internal Revenue Service
lower left, Department of Justice
upper right, F.B.I. Building
lower right, Petersen House where Lincoln was taken after
being shot in the Ford Theatre.

En haut, à gauche: Service Interne du Revenu
En bas, à gauche: Département de la Justice
En haut, à droite: Bâtiment du F.B.I.
En bas, à droite: Petersen House où Lincoln fut transporté
après avoir été abattu au Théâtre Ford.

oben links: Finanzamt für Innere Angelegenheiten
unten links: Justizministerium
oben rechts: F.B.I. - Gebäude
unten rechts: Petersen Haus. Hierher wurde Lincoln ge-
bracht, nachdem er im Ford Theater erschossen worden
war.

arriba a la izquierda, Servicio de Renta Interna
abajo a la izquierda, Departamento de Justicia
arriba a la derecha, Edificio del F.B.I.
abajo a la derecha, la Petersen House a donde fué llevado
Lincoln después de que le habían disparado en el Teatro
Ford.

Ford Theatre in which President Lincoln was assassin
ted on April 14, 1865.

Teatro Ford, en el que fué asesinado Lincoln el 14
Abril de 1865.

Le Théâtre Ford où le Président Lincoln fut assassiné
14 Avril 1865.

Das Ford Theater, wo Präsident Lincoln am 14. Ap
1865 ermordet wurde.

Columned portico of the Post Office Department and the Department of Labor. Below, The old Post Office Building.

Portique à colonnades du Département des Services Postaux et le Département du Travail. Au-dessous, l'ancien Edifice des Services Postaux.

Säulengang des Post- und Arbeitsministeriums. Darunter: das ehemalige Hauptpostgebäude.

Pórtico con columnas del Departamento de Correos y Departamento del Trabajo. Abajo, el antiguo Edificio de Correos.

upper left, District Building
upper right, U.S. Department of Lab
lower right, Department of Commer

En haut, a gauche: L'Edifice Région
En haut, à droite: Le Départemen
Travail des Etats Unis
En bas, à droite: Le Département
Commerce

unten links: Bezirksamt
oben rechts: Arbeitsministerium
Vereinigten Staaten
unten rechts: Handelsministerium

arriba a la izquierda, Edificio del
stricto
arriba a la derecha, Departamento
Trabajo de los EE.UU.
abajo a la derecha, Departamento
Comercio.

Looking down Pennsylvania Avenue toward the impressive United States Capitol.

Vue du Capitole des Etats Unis à travers l'Avenue Pennsylvania.

Blick von der Pennsylvania Avenue auf das eindrucksvolle Kapitol der Vereinten Staaten.

Mirando hacia abajo desde la Pennsylvania Avenue hacia el impresionante Capitolio de los Estados Unidos.

The Treasury Department at left, and right, General Sherman Statue at Hamilton Place.

A gauche, le Département de la Trésorerie et, à droite, la Statue du Général Sherman sur la Place Hamilton.

Links das Schatzministerium und rechts das Denkmal des General Sherman am Hamilton-Platz.

A la izquierda el Departamento del Tesoro, y a la derecha la estatua del General Sherman en la Plaza Hamilton.

Washington Monument. Construction of the Monument was begun in 1848 and was completed in 1884, 85 years after the death of Washington in 1799. The white marble shaft rises 555 feet and stands on the Mall, between the Lincoln Memorial and the Capitol.

Monument Washington. La construction du Monument commença en 1848 et fut achevée en 1884, 85 ans après la mort de Washington en 1799. La colonne en marbre blanc s'élève à une hauteur de 555 pieds et se dresse sur le Mall entre le Mémorial Lincoln et le Capitole.

Das Washington Monument. Die Errichtung dieses gigantischen Denkmals wurde Im Jahre 1848 begonnen und 1884 fertiggestellt - 85 Jahre nach dem Tod von George Washington im Jahre 1799. Der weisse Marmorobelisk erreicht eine Höbe von 555 Fuss und befindet sich am Mall genau in der Mitte zwischen der Lincoln-Gedächtnisstätte und dem Kapitol.

Monumento a Washington. La construcción del Monumento se comenzó en 1848 y fué completada en 1884, 85 años después de la muerte de Washington en 1799. La columna de mármol blanco alcanza los 555 pies y está situada sobre el Mall, entre el monumento e la memoria de Lincoln y el Capitolio.

Jefferson Memorial. The Memorial, designed by John Russel Pope, was dedicated in 1943. The classic style reflects Jefferson's own taste in architecture and bears a marked resemblance to Monticello, his home in Virginia.

Mémorial Jefferson. Le Monument commémoratif, réalisé par John Russel Pope fut consacré en 1943. Le style classique reflète le goût architectural de Jefferson lui-même et ressemble beaucoup à Monticello, sa demeure en Virginie.

Das Jefferson Denkmal. Dieses Denkmal, entworfen von John Russel, wurde im Jahre 1943 eingeweiht. Der klassische Baustil entspricht Jefferson's eigenem Geschmack hinsichtlich Architektur und hat in vielem unverkennbare Ähnlichkeiten mit Monticello, seinem Landhaus in Virginia.

Monumento a la memoria de Jefferson. El Monumento, diseñado por John Russel Pope, fué dedicado en 1943. El estilo clásico refleja el propio gusto de Jefferson en cuanto se refiere a arquitectura y tiene un parecido notable con Monticello, su casa en Virginia.

Two of the many picturesque views from the top of the Washington Monument. The Constitution Gardens and the United States Capitol.

Deux des nombreuses vues pittoresques du haut du Monument à Washington: les Jardins de la Constitution et le Capitole des Etats Unis.

Zwei der unzähligen malerischen Ausblicke, die man von der Spitze des Washington Monuments aus geniessen kann: die Gartenanlagen des Regierungspalastes und das Kapitol der Vereinigten Staaten.

Dos de las muchas vistas pintorescas desde la cima del Monumento a Washington. Los Jardines de la Constitución y el Capitolio de los Estados Unidos.

The White House has the simple elegance
of a gracious American home, it reflects
the design of manor houses in Ireland,
England and France.
top left The Red Room, one of the four
state reception rooms.
top right, The oval Blue Room with many
of the furnishings in the French Empire
style,
bottom left, the Green Room, a first-floor
reception room.
bottom center, The State Dining Room.
bottom right, The East Room, largest and
most formal of the state reception rooms,
remaining unfinished until 1829.

La Maison Blanche possède l'élégance
simple d'une gracieuse maison Américaine et reflète le dessin des maisons résidentielles Irlandaises, Anglaises et Françaises.
En haut à gauche, la Chambre Rouge,
une des quatre chambres pour les récep-
tions d'Etat.
En haut à droite, la Chambre Bleue ovale
avec una grande partie de l'ameublement
en style Empire Français,
En bas è gauche, la Chambre Verte, une
chambre de réception au premier étage.
En bas au centre, La Salle à Manger
d'Etat.
En bas à droite, La Chambre Est, la plus
grande et la plus conventionnelle des
chambres de réception, restée inachevée
jusqu'à 1829.

Das Weisse Haus hat die einfache Eleganz
eines amerikanischen Hauses und ähnelt
in seinem Aussehen einem herrschaftlichen
Landhaus aus Irland, England oder Frank-
reich.
Oben links, das Rote Zimmer, eines der
vier Zimmer, die den Staatsempfängen
dienen.
Oben rechts, das Blaue Zimmer, oval mit
einem grossen Teil der Einrichtung im
französischen Empire-Stil;
Unten links, das Grüne Zimmer, ein Emp-
fangszimmer im ersten Stock.
Unten Mitte, das Staatsspeisezimmer. Auf
Unten rechts, das Ost-Zimmer ist das
grösste und das förmlichste Empfangs-
zimmer; es blied bis 1829 unvollendet.

La Casa Blanca posee la elegancia sencilla de una graciosa casa Americana y
refleja el diseño de las casas señoriales
Irlandesas, Inglesias y Francesas.
Arriba a la izquierda, la Habitación Roja,
una de las cuatro habitaciones para las
recepciones de Estado.
Arriba a la derecha, la Habitación Azul
ovalada con gran parte de la decoración
en estilo Imperio Francés,
Abajo a la izquierda, la Habitación Verde,
una habitación de recepción en el primer
piso.
Abajo en el centro, la Habitación Comedor
de Estado.
Abajo a la derecha, la Habitación Este,
la más grande y la más formal de las
habitaciones de receptión que quedara
sin terminar hasta 1829.

The Executive Office Building presently is a part of the Executive Office of the President. At one time President Taft's cow, Pauline, used the park behind the building as her pasture. At bottom is the First Division Monument "Victory". In the lower right is the War Memorial, U.S. Army Second Division.

L'Edifice des Bureaux Administratifs fait, actuellement, partie du Bureau du Président. A une certaine période la vache du Président Taft broutait dans le Parc qui se trouvait derrière l'édifice.
En bas, le monument "Victory" dédié à la Première Division. En bas, à droite, le monument élevé à la Mémoire des soldats de la Deuxième Division de l'Armée des Etats Unis.

Das Burogebäude der Staatspolizei ist zur Zeit ein Teil des Polizeibüros des Präsidenten. Seinerzeit verwendete die Kuh von Präsident Taft, Pauline genannt, den hinteren Teil des Parks als Weidefläche. Unten befindet sich das Denkmal der Ersten Division "der Sieg". Rechts unten befindet sich ein Kriegsdenkmal zu Ehren der Zweiten Division der Armee der Vereinigten Staaten.

El Edificio de la Oficina del Ejecutivo forma parte actualmente de la Oficina del Ejecutivo del Presidente. Hubo una época en la que la vaca del Presidente Taft, Pauline, usaba el parque situado detrás del edificio como pasto. En la parte más baja está el Monumento de la Primera División "Victoria". Abajo, a la derecha, se encuentra el monumento en conmemoración de la Guerra de la Segunda División del Ejército de los EE.UU.

The South Portico of the White House. The White House was burned by the British in 1814, but was rebuilt and received its porticos in the 1820s.

Le Portique sud de la Maison Blanche. La Maison Blanche fut incendiée par les Anglais en 1814 et reconstruite, avec ses portiques, au cours des années 1820.

Der Säulengang an der Südfassade des Weissen Hauses. Das Weisse Haus wurde im Jahre 1814 von den Engländern niedergebrannt, wurde aber in den Zwanzigerjahren des 19. Jahrhunderts wieder aufgebaut und erhielt damals seine Säulengänge.

El Pórtico Sur de la Casa Blanca. La Casa Blanca fué incendiada por los Ingleses en 1814, pero fué reconstruida y se le añadieron los pórticos en los años 1820.

Top, Blair House, official "guest house" of the U.S. and bottom, Decatur House adjoining Truxtun-Decatur Naval Museum. Both are located at Lafayette Park.

En haut, Blair House, la "Maison des invités" officiels des Etats Unis; en bas, Decatur House contiguë au Musée Naval Truxtun-Decatur. Les deux Edifices se dressent dans le Parc Lafayette.

Oben: das Blair-Haus, das offizielle Gästehaus der Vereinigten Staaten und unten das Decatur-Haus, das an das Trunxtun-Decatur - Marine Museum anschliesst. Beide liegen direkt am Lafayette Park.

Arriba, Blair House, "casa de huéspedes" oficial de los EE.UU. y abajo la Decatur House lindante con el Museo Naval Truxtun-Decatur. Ambos están situados en el Parque de Lafayette.

base of Kosciuszko Statue, St.
n's Church and Jackson Statue
Lafayette Park.

soubassement de la Statue Ko-
uszko, l'Eglise St. Jean et la Sta-
de Jackson au Parc Lafayette.

Sockel der Kosciuszko Statue,
Kirche des Heiligen Johannes
das Jackson Denkmal beim La-
ette Park.

base de la Estatua Kosciuszko,
sia de St. John y la Estatua de
kson en el Parque de Lafayette.

Right, Memorial Continental Hall D.A.R. Its Museum contains many old treasures.

A droite, le Monument commémoratif Continental Hall D.A.R. Son musée, où sont exposés de nombreux vieux trésors.

Rechts: Die Memorial Continental Halle D.A.R. Sein Museum enthält unzählige alte Schätze.

A la derecha, Salón Continental Conmemorativo D.A.R. Su Museo contiene muchos tesoros antiguos.

Top left, The Pan American Union, headquarters of the Organization of American States.
Bottom left, Corcoran Gallery of Art. Exhibits include old masters, contemporary works and antique furnishings.
Bottom right, American National Red Cross, National Headquarters.

En haut, à gauche, l'Union Panaméricaine, quartiers généraux de l'Organisation des Etats Américains. En bas, à gauche, la Galerie d'Art Corcoran. Les objets exposés comprennent des œuvres de vieux maîtres, des travaux contemporains et des meubles antiques. En bas, à droite, la Croix Rouge Nationale Américaine, Quartiers Généraux Nationaux.

Oben links: Die Panamerikanische Union; Organisationshauptsitz für die amerikanischen Staaten. Links unten: Die Corcoran Kunstgalerie. Die Ausstellungsstücke reichen von Gemälden alter Meister über zeitgenössische Kunst zu antiken Mobelstücken. Rechts unten: Das Amerikanische Rote Kreuz, Hauptsitz der Nation.

Arriba a la izquierda, la Unión Pan Americana, cuartel general de la Organización de los Estados Americanos.
Abajo a la izquierda, Galería de Arte Corcoran. Expone antiguas obras maestras, obras contemporáneas y muebles antiguos.
Abajo a la derecha, Cruz Roja Nacional Americana, Cuartel general Nacional.

Lincoln Memorial. This 19-foot-high marble statue of the seated Lincoln was executed by Daniel Chester French and is located inside the Memorial. Incribed above the statue are the words:

IN THIS TEMPLE
AS IN THE HEARTS OF THE PEOPLE
FOR WHOM HE SAVED THE UNION
THE MEMORY OF ABRAHAM LINCOLN
IS ENSHRINED FOREVER

Mémorial à Lincoln. Cette statue en marbre de 19 pieds de hauteur, représentant Lincoln assis, fut réalisée par Daniel Chester French; elle est placée à l'intérieur du Mémorial. On peut lire au-dessus de la statue:

DANS CE TEMPLE
COMME DANS LES COEURS DES HOMMES
POUR LESQUELS IL SAUVA L'UNION
LE SOUVENIR D'ABRAHAM LINCOLN
RESTE A TOUT JAMAIS GRAVÉ

Die Lincoln-Gedächtnisstätte. Diese 19 Fuss hohe Marmorstatue zeigt den sitzenden Präsidenten Lincoln; sie wurde von Daniel Chester French gemeisselt und im Inneren des Monumentes aufgestellt. Uber der Statue sind folgende Worte auf einer Inschrifttafel graviert:

IN DIESEM TEMPEL
SOWIE IN DEN HERZEN DER BEVÖLKERUNG
UM DERENTWILLEN ER DIE
UNION GERETTET HAT
IST DAS ANDENKEN AN ABRAHAM LINCOLN
FÜR EWIG FESTGEHALTEN.

Monumento a la Memoria de Lincoln. Esta estatua de Mármol de 19 pies del altura que representa a Lincoln sentado, fué realizada por Daniel Chester French y esté situada dentro del Memorial. Sobre la estatua están grabadas las siguientes palabras:

EN ESTE TEMPLO
COMO EN LOS CORAZONES DE LAS PERSONAS
PARA LAS CUALES SALVÓ A LA UNIÓN
EL RECUERDO DE ABRAHAM LINCOLN
SE CONSERVA COMO UNA RELIQUIA
PARA SIEMPRE.

The memorial to our 16th President, Abraham Lincoln, is a white marble building of classic design, resembling the Parthenon of Greece. It was designed by Henry Bacon and completed in 1922. Facing the Lincoln Memorial on the West side are these massive statues given to the people of the United States by the people of Italy.

Le mémorial au 16ème Président, Abraham Lincoln, est un édifice en marbre blanc de réalisation classique, qui rappelle le Panthéon de Grèce. Il fut conçu par Henry Bacon et achevé en 1922. En face du Mémorial à Lincoln, à l'ouest, se trouvent les statues massives, don du peuple Italien au peuple Américain.

Das Denkmal, das unserem 16. Prasidenten Abraham Lincoln gewidmet ist, ein weisses Marmorgebäude in klassischer Linienfuehrung und erinnert uns an den Parthenon von Griechenland Die Entwürfe stammen von Henry Bacon; der Bau wurde im Jahre 1922 beendet. Die massiven Steinstatuen, die der Lincoln-Gedachtnisstette an der Westseite gegenüberstehen sind der amerikanischen Bevölkerung vom italienischen Volk geschenkt worden.

El monumento a la memoria del nuestro decimosexto Presidente, Abraham Lincoln, es un edificio de mármol blanco de diseño clásico, parecido al partenón de Grecia. Fué diseñado por Henry Bacon y completado en 1922. Enfrente al Monumento a Lincoln en la parte oeste se encuentran las imponentes estatuas regaladas al pueblo de los Estados Unidos por el pueblo de Italia.

Top, John F. Kennedy Center for the Performing Arts. Designed by Edward Durell Stone, the memorial is located on the banks of the Potomac. Its facilities include an opera house, a concert hall and two large theaters.
Bottom left, Watergate Hotel.
Bottom right, Starplex Robert F. Kennedy Memorial Stadium. The Stadium accommodates professional baseball and football teams as well as numerous college activities.

En haut, Centre John F. Kennedy pour l'Accomplissement des Arts.
Dessiné par Edward Durell Stone, le Mémorial est situé sur les rives du Potomac. Il contient un théàtre lyrique, une salle de concerts et deux grandes salles de cinéma.
En bas, à gauche, le Watergate Hotel.

Oben: Das Hohn F. Kennedy Center fur die darstellenden Künste.
Dieses von Edward Durell Stone entworfene Gebäude liegt am Unfer des Potoma-Flusses. Seine Räumlichkeiten beinhalten eine Oper, eine Konzerthalle und zwei riesige Theatersale. Links unten: das Watergate Hote. Rechts unten: Das Starplex Robert F. Kennedy Gedächtnis Stadion. Dieses Stadion bietet professionellen Basketball-und Fussballteams und anderen zahlreichen.

Arriba, el Centro John F. Kennedy para las Artes Representativas. Diseñado por Edward Durell Stone, el monumento conmemorativo está situado a las orillas del Potomac.
Sus instalaciones incluyen a una ópera, un salón de conciertos y dos amplios teatros.
Abajo, a la izquierda, Hotel. Watergate.
Abajo, a la derecha, Estadio conmemorativo Starplex Robert F. Kennedy. El Estadio aloja a equipos profesionales de beísbol y de fútbol así como a numerosas actividades de universitarios.

Georgetown, now a part of Washington, was first settled in the 17th century. It has been carefully restored and has become one of the most exclusive residential sections in Washington. The historic C. & O. Canal, which counted George Washington as one of its investors, was opened in the 1820s. At bottom is the oldest house in the Washington area, the Old Stone House, built in 1766 as the home and shop of a cabinetmaker.

Georgetown fait désormais partie de Washington; elle fut construite au 17ème siècle. Elle a été restaurée avec beaucoup de soins et elle est actuellement l'une des zones les plus exlusivement résidentielles de Washington. Le Canal historique C. & O. dont George Washington fut l'un des actionnaires, fut ouvert dans les années 1820. En bas, la plus vieille maison à Washington, la Old Stone House (la vieille maison de pierre) bâtie en 1766 pour servir de demeure et d'atelier à un ébéniste.

Georgetown, heute ein Stadtteil von Washington, wurde bereits im 17. Jahrhundert gegründet. Es wurde sorgfältig restauriert und ist somit zu einer der exklusivsten Wohngegenden von Washington geworden. Der historische C. & O.-Kanal, der hauptsächlich mit von George Washington aufgebrachten Mitteln gebaut werden konnte, wurde im Jahre 1820 eröffnet. An seinem unteren Ende befindet sich das älteste Haus von ganz Washington und Umgebung: the Old Stone House, 1766 als Wohnsitz und Geschäft eines Kunsttischlers errichtet.

Georgetown, actualmente una parte de Washington, fué fundada por primera vez en el siglo XVII. Ha sido restaurada cuidadosamente y se ha convertido en una de las zonas residenciales más exclusivas de Washington. El histórico Canal C. & O., que tuvo a George Washington como uno de sus inversores, fué abierto en los años 1820. En la parte de abajo se encuentra la casa más antigua de la zona de Washington, la Old Stone House, construida en 1766 como la casa y tienda de un ebanista.

Arlington Memorial Bridge was proposed by Daniel Webster and considered by Congress in 1851, approved in 1925, and completed in 1932.

Arlington Memorial Bridge (Pont Commémoratif d'Arlington); il fut réalisé par Daniel Webster, étudié par le Congrès en 1851, approuvé en 1925 et achevé en 1932.

Die Arlington-Gedächtnis-Brücke wurde von Daniel Webster entworfen, im Jahre 1851 vom Kongress in Erwägung gezogen; 1925 akzeptiert und 1932 vollendet.

Puente Conmemorativo de Arlington: fué propuesto por Daniel Webster y considerado por el Congreso en 1851, aprobado en 1925, y completado en 1932.

Tomb of the Unknown Soldier in Arlington Cemetery. Day and night, a lone sentry paces back and forth before this tomb, whose incription reads: «Here rests in honored glory an American Soldier, known but to God».

Tombeau du Soldat Inconnu au Cimetière d'Arlington. Nuit et jour une sentinelle monte la garde devant le tombeau, sur lequel l'on peut lire: «Ci-gît, honoré dans sa gloire, un Soldat Américain, connu seulement par Dieu».

Das Grab des Unbekannten Soldaten am Heldenfriedhof von Arlington. Vor diesem Grab patrouilliert Tag und Nacht eine einsame Wache auf und ab; die Inschrift dort besagt Folgendes: «Hier ruht in ewiger Verehrung ein amerikanischer Soldat, den Gott allein kennt».

Tumba del Soldado Desconocido en el Cementerio de Arlington. Día y noche, un centinela solitario desfila de un lado al otro delante de esta tumba, cuya inscripción dice: «Aquí descansa en digna gloria un Soldado Americano, que sólo Dios conoce».

Arlington Memorial Amphi-
theatre has a seating capa-
city of about 5.000.

Amphithéâtre Commémora-
tif d'Arlington; il peut rece-
voir environ 5000 personnes
assises.

Das Arlington-Gedächtnis-
Amphitheater fasst Sitz-
plätze für ungefähr 5000 Zu-
schauer.

Anfiteatro Conmemorativo
de Arlington, que tiene una
capacidad de asientos de
aproximadamente 5.000.

John F. Kennedy Grave.
Here burns the eternal flame
which was lighted during
the burial service.

Le tombeau de John F. Kennedy. Ici la flamme éternelle
brûle, qui avait été allumée
au cours du service funèbre.

Das Grab von John F. Ken-
nedy. Hier brennt ein Ewiges
Licht, das seinerzeit während der Begräbnisfeierlich-
keit entzündet wurde.

Tumba de John F. Kennedy.
Aquí arde la llama eterna
que fué encendida durante
el funeral.

Right, Arlington House, R.E. Lee Mansion.
Bottom, U.S. Marine Corps War Memorial. Felix W. De Weldon's masterpiece depicts one of the most dramatic events of World War II, the raising of the Stars and Stripes on Mt. Suribachi, Iwo Jima. Dedicated November 10, 1954, it is the largest sculpture ever cast in bronze.

A droite, Arlington House, R.E. Lee Mansion.
En bas, le Mémorial de Guerre dédié au Corps de la Marine Américaine; le chef-d'œuvre de Félix W. Weldon, évoque l'un des évènements les plus dramatiques de la IIe Guerre Mondiale: la montée de la bannière étoilée sur le Mont Suribachi à Iwo Jima. Consacré le 10 Novembre 1954, il constitue la plus grande sculpture qui ait été jamais coulée en bronze.

Rechts: Das Arlington Haus, das Landhaus von R.E. Lee. Unten: Das Kriegerdenkmal der Marine der Vereinigten Staaten. Dieses Meisterwerk, geschaffen von Felix W. De Weldon, stellt eines der dramatischsten Ereignisse des zweiten Weltkrieges dar: das Hissen des Banners mit den Sternen und den Streifen am Mount Suribachi, Iwo Jima; Dieses am 10. November 1954 enthüllte Denkmal ist die grösste Skulptur, die je in Bronze gegossen wurde.

A la derecha, Arlington House, Mansión de R.E. Lee Abajo, Monumento Conmemorativo a la Guerra Cuerpo de Marines de los EE.UU. La obra maestra Felix W. De Weldon's representa uno de los más d maticos sucesos de la segunda Guerra Mundial, el zamiento de la bandera americana sobre el monte S bachi, Iwo Jima. Dedicado el 10 de Noviembre de 195 es la escultura más grande que se haya producido bronce en todos los tiempos.

Washington Cathedral, officially the Cathedral Church of St. Peter and St. Paul, one of the world's sixth largest ecclesiastical edifices.

La Cathédrale de Washington, officiellement la Cathédrale Eglise de St. Pierre et St. Paul, le sixième plus grand édifice écclésiastique du monde.

Die Kathedrale von Washington - ihr offizieller Name lautet die Kirche der Heiligen Petrus und Paulus - ist der sechstgrösste Sakralbau auf der ganzen Welt.

Catedral de Washington, oficialmente la Catedral Iglesia de San Pedro y San Pablo, uno de los seís mayores edificios eclesiásticos del mundo.

National Shrine of the Immaculate Conception is the tribute of American Catholics to Our Blessed Mother as Patroness of the Country.

La Chapelle Nationale de l'Immaculée Conception est l'hommage des Catholiques Américains à Notre Sainte Mère, protectrice de la Nation.

Ein der Unbefleckten Empfängnis gewidmetes Nationaldenkmal ist der Beitrag der amerikanischen Katholiken zur Verehrung der heiligen Muttergottes, der Schutzpatronin des Landes.

La Capilla Nacional de la Inmaculada Concepción es el tributo de los Católicos Americanos a nuestra Bendita Madre, como Patrona del país.

Pentagon Building, Arlington, Virginia. The five-sided giant, nerve center of the Defense Department is the largest office building in the world.

L'Edifice du Pentagone, Arlington, Virginie. Ce géant à cinq bras, centre nerveux du Département de la Défense, est le bâtiment-bureau le plus grand au monde.

Das Pentagon Gebäude in Arlington, Virginia. Diese fünfeckige riesige Gehirnzelle des Verteidigunsministeriums ist das grösste Burogebäude in der ganzen Welt.

Edificio del Pentagono, Arlington, Virginia. El gigante de cinco lados, nervio central del Departamento de la Defensa es el mayor edificio de oficinas del mundo.

National Geographic Society. As headquarters of the largest scientific and educational organization in the world, it is here that all of the Society's exploration projects are planned and the National Geographic Magazine is prepared. In Explorers Hall, there are mementos and trophies from famed Geographic expeditions.

Société Nationale de Géographie. Quartier Général de la plus grande organisation scientifique et d'enseignement au monde; c'est ici que tous les projets d'exploration de la Société sont étudiés et mis au point et que la Revue Nationale de Géographie est préparée. Dans la Salle des Explorateurs, souvenirs et trophées des plus célèbres expéditions.

Die Nationale Geographiche Gesellschaft. In diesem Hauptzitz der grössten wissenschaftlichen-und Bildungsorganisation der Welt werden alle von der Gesellschaft in Erwägung gezogene Forschungsprojekte geplant und es wird die Monatszeitschrift "National Geographic" vorbereitet und gedruckt. In der sogenannten "Forscherhalle" werden die wichtigsten Erinnerungsstücke und Trophäen von den berühmtesten Expeditionen aufbewahrt.

Sociedad Geográfica Nacional. Como cuartel general de la mayor organización científica y educativa del mundo, aquí es donde se planean todos lor proyectos de exploración de la Sociedad y donde se prepara la Revista Geográfica Nacional. En el Salón de los Exploradores hay recuerdos y trofeos de famosas expediciones.

Mount Vernon, the home of George Washington, is beautifully situated on the west bank of the Potomac River, 15 miles south of Washington, D.C. It was erected about 1743 by Lawrence Washington, half-brother of the First President. George Washington subsequently inherited the estate with thousands of acres of rolling land. It was the family seat until 1860, when it was purchased by the Mount Vernon Ladies Association, as a national shrine.

Le Mont Vernon, demeure de George Washington, est merveilleusement située sur la rive occidentale du Fleuve Potomac, à 15 miles au sud de Washington, D.C. Elle fut construite vers 1743 par Lawrence Washington, demi-frère de Premier Président. George Washington hérita, par la suite, de la propriété avec des milliers d'acres de terres ondulées. Elle demeura le siège de la famille jusqu'en 1860, lorsqu'elle fut achetée par l'Association des Dames de Mont Vernon, comme lieu de consécration.

Mount Vernon, der Wohnzitz von George Washington, befindet sich in zauberhafter Lage am Westufer des Potomac Flusses 15 Meilen südlich von Washington D.C. Es wurde um das Jahr 1743 von Lawrence Washington, dem Halbbruder des ersten Präsidenten, erbaut. In der Folge erbte es dann George Washington: einen Landitz mit tausenden Acker bewirtschafteten Landes. Es blieb bis zum Jahr 1860 Familiensitz der Washington, bis es dann von der Gesellschaft der Damen von Mount Vernon abgekauft wurde und heute wie ein Nationaldenkmal verehrt wird.

Mount Vernon, la casa de George Washington, está bellísimamente situada en la orilla oeste del Rio Potomac, a 15 millas al sur de Washington, D.C. Fué erigida alrededor del 1743 por Lawrence Washington, medio hermano del Primer Presidente. George Washington heredó sucesivamente la propiedad con miles de acres de tierra ondulada. Esta fué la sede de la familia hasta 1860, cuando fué comprada por la Asociación de Mujeres de Mount Vernon, como una reliquia nacional.

After Washington's death, in 1799, he was buried in a simple vault southeast of the house. His remains and those of Mrs. Washington were later reinterred in the present tomb, west of the old grave site.

Après sa mort en 1799, Washington fut enterré dans un caveau simple, au sud-est de la maison. Ses restes et ceux de Mme Washington furent plus tard transférés dans la tombe actuelle dans le vieux cimitière.

Nach seinem Tod im Jahre 1799 wurde George Washington in einem ganz bescheidenem Grab südöstlich des Hauses beigesetzt. Seine und die sterblichen Überreste seiner Frau wurden später exhumiert und in der heutigen Gruft westlich von der ehemaligen Begräbnisstelle beigesetzt.

Trás la muerte de Washington, en 1799, éste fué enterrado en una sencilla bóveda la sureste de la casa. Sus restos y los de la Sra. Washington fueron más tarde enterrados de nuevo en la tumba actual, al oeste del lugar que ocupaba la antigua tumba.